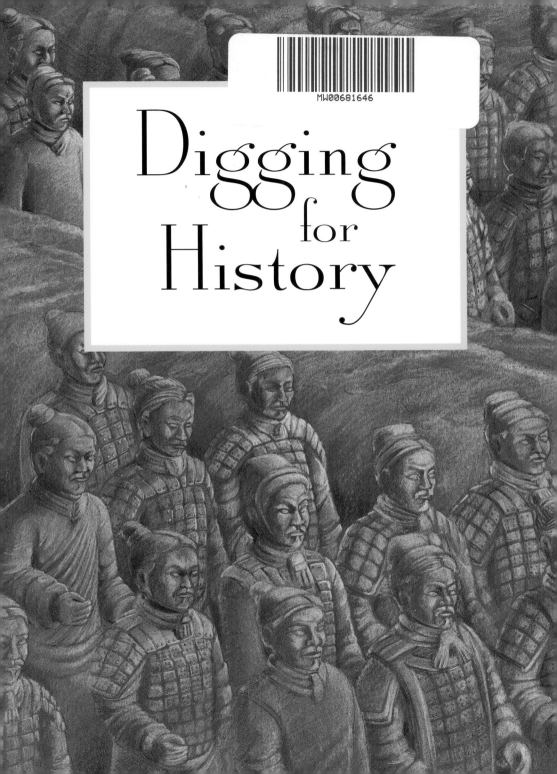

Digging
for
History

Contents

Features

WORD BUILDER

What do the two parts of the word *archaeology* mean? Turn to page 4 for the answer, and then try to figure out the meaning of some more "arch" words.

PROFILE

Who made an amazing archaeological discovery in 1978? Find out in **Famous for Footprints** on page 10.

IN FOCUS

What really caused the *Titanic* to sink? Discover more in **An Underwater Mystery** on page 14.

TRY THIS!

Do you know that there is a way of making sure people in the future will know who you were and how you lived? Read **Make Your Own Time Capsule** on page 29.

SITESEEING · SCIENCE & TECHNOLOGY

How do archaeologists dig up the truth?
Visit www.rigbyinfoquest.com
for more about ARCHAEOLOGY.

What Is Archaeology?

Archaeology is the study of human history through the **analysis** of buried remains from the past. Scientists who study these remains are called archaeologists. By looking carefully at remains, or artifacts, we can learn about what took place long ago. An awareness of the past helps us to understand the present and plan for the future.

The people who lived thousands of years ago at Akrotiri, on Santorini in Greece, had to flee their town because of strong earthquakes. Volcanic material from the eruption of a volcano then covered the town and **preserved** the buildings and their contents. Many of the ancient objects uncovered at Akrotiri today are still whole.

WORD BUILDER

The word *archaeology* is made up of two parts. *Arche* means "the beginning" and *–ology* means "the study of." See if you can guess what these other "arch" words mean: *archaic, archetype,* and *archives.* Then look them up in the dictionary to see if your guesses were correct.

Ancient Greek vase showing olive harvesters

Roman coin of the two-faced god Janus

Babylonian tablet recording sky observations

Answers in Artifacts

Artifacts are objects made or used by humans. There are two main kinds of artifacts. The first includes pottery, weapons, tools, and coins. A second type, called **epigraphs,** includes ancient writing, inscriptions, and even graffiti!

ΑΒΓΔΕΖΗΘΙΚΛΜΝΞΟΠΡΣΤΥΦΧΨΩ

There were 24 letters in the ancient Greek alphabet.

Archaeology is not just a matter of digging up artifacts, however. Research before and after a dig takes much time and effort. The work is often long and difficult, but it can be very rewarding.

Dig This!

Where to Look

Some artifacts are easy to find because they are above ground. Many, however, are buried beneath the surface of Earth or hidden deep in overgrown jungles. Some are even lying beneath the sea in shipwrecks from ancient times. How, then, do archaeologists know where to look? The starting point is often a local story or a historical record.

Today, archaeologists, students, and volunteers are working to excavate the lost city of Ubar, in Oman. The city wasn't found until the 1980s when an American archaeologist enlisted NASA's help. Remote sensing satellites uncovered caravan tracks in the desert that all led to one place. The city that had been lost for thousands of years was found!

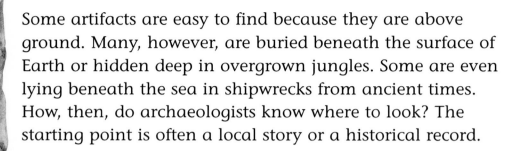

United Arab Emirates

Saudi Arabia

OMAN

Yemen

Archaeologists are careful when brushing away dirt and debris at a dig. They have to make sure they do not damage the artifacts that they find.

Once a possible site is located, archaeologists must get permission from those who own the land to start a dig. The site may be several square miles in area, so careful planning of where to begin is important. The first step is to carefully **survey** the whole site, taking care not to disturb or destroy any artifacts in the process.

Digging at a Site

Once a possible site has been discovered and permission to dig given, the archaeology team is ready to begin. The following are some important steps in a dig.

Step 1

The Plan
Measurements are taken so that a site map can be made. Square grid lines are then drawn on the map.

Step 2

Mapping the Area
The map is used to divide the site into squares. The squares are marked with string and wooden posts.

Step 3

Removing Soil
The topsoil of one section of the grid is carefully removed and set aside.

Step 4

The Dig

Archaeologists then use trowels and other tools to carefully dig and remove artifacts.

Step 5

Gathering Evidence

The removed soil is sifted for tiny bits of history. All artifacts and the dig site are photographed or videotaped.

Step 6

Analysis

Back in the lab, the artifacts are examined to see what they reveal about the history of the area.

Famous for Footprints

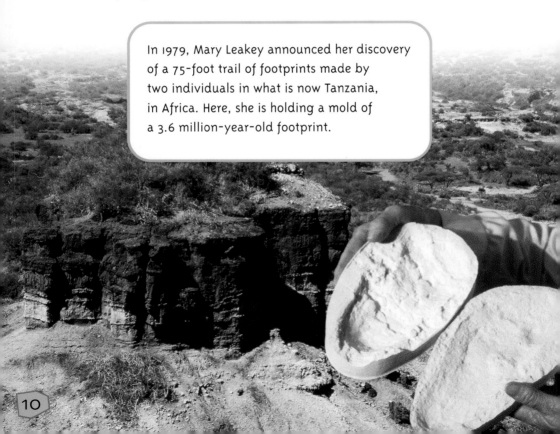

Mary Leakey (1913–1996)

Mary Leakey was one of the most famous archaeologists and **anthropologists** of the twentieth century. Born in England as Mary Nicol, she was taught to read and draw by her father. He also introduced her to anthropology. Mary's free spirit and disregard of rules caused her to be expelled from two schools. She did not have the qualifications necessary to follow her dream of studying anthropology at a university. However, Mary didn't give up. She began sitting in on lectures at universities and museums and helping at archaeological digs.

In 1979, Mary Leakey announced her discovery of a 75-foot trail of footprints made by two individuals in what is now Tanzania, in Africa. Here, she is holding a mold of a 3.6 million-year-old footprint.

Mary then traveled to Africa with her husband, who was an archaeologist. Without any formal training, she made some of the most important discoveries of all time. This included her find, in 1978, of the oldest human footprints yet discovered. In a time when many female scientists found it difficult to get recognition, Mary's hard work and dedication were successful.

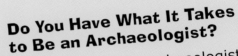

Do You Have What It Takes to Be an Archaeologist?

Today, successful archaeologists need a good education as well as the following skills.

Patience: Exploring a complete site can take a long time.

People skills: Archaeologists must be able to communicate clearly with others.

Literacy skills: The ability to read and write a variety of documents and reports is important.

Analytical skills: The ability to interpret and understand the artifacts found is important.

Physical fitness: Because living on site can be hard work, fitness is important.

Uncovering Secrets

Finding Fossils

Paleontologists are scientists who uncover and study dinosaur fossils. By careful study, paleontologists can tell when dinosaurs lived and how they looked. Putting together fossils to construct a complete dinosaur is a long and difficult job. It is like putting together a jigsaw puzzle without the picture for reference.

Dinosaur Dating

How do we know when dinosaurs lived and when they died out? There are two main ways of finding out.

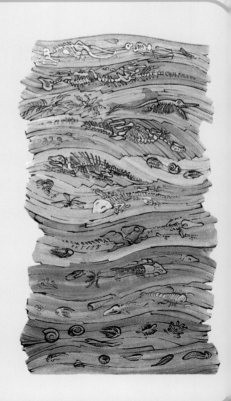

1. We can figure out the age of a fossil by figuring out the age of the rock in which it is found. This can be done because **radioactive** rocks decay at a steady rate.

2. The depth at which fossils are found can tell us how old they are. Fossils that are buried deep in **sedimentary** rock are usually older than fossils that are buried closer to the surface.

Many scientists think that dinosaurs first appeared about 240 million years ago and died out about 65 million years ago.

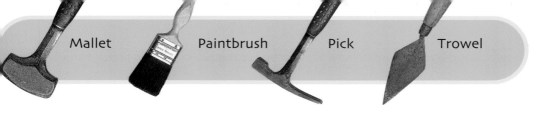

Mallet   Paintbrush   Pick   Trowel

When the fossils are finally arranged, paleontologists can imagine what the dinosaur looked like. They can figure out how it moved, what it ate, and how it protected itself. However, there is also much information that can't be discovered. We have no way of knowing what color dinosaurs were or what sounds they made.

Artifacts are placed on trays and lifted to the surface by balloonlike bags.

Archaeologists who work underwater use many of the same methods as archaeologists who work on land. However, underwater sites often require special equipment. Artificial lighting is needed because there is no natural light underwater. If the shipwreck is far underwater, submersibles are used to transport the archaeology team to the site.

Wrecks and Treasures

In ancient times, many ships were wrecked because dangerous voyages were made in uncharted seas. The crews of these ships often had poor navigational skills. Trading ships at this time carried goods such as timber, ivory, glass, cloth, and pottery jars of oil and grain. Today, these artifacts provide archaeologists with important clues about people of the past and their customs.

As they do on land, archaeologists use an excavation grid to mark off areas of the ocean floor and then record what they find in each square. They use both cameras and video cameras to make accurate records. The most important equipment for underwater archaeologists, however, is scuba-dive gear. This allows them to dive to great depths and stay underwater for about an hour at a time, using one tank of air.

An Underwater Mystery

One of the most famous shipwrecks is the sunken passenger liner *Titanic.* It hit an iceberg on its first voyage across the Atlantic Ocean in 1912 and sank. Many people had believed the *Titanic* was unsinkable because of its design. The hull had 16 separate watertight compartments. It was thought that even if two of these compartments flooded, the ship would stay afloat. However, when the ship hit the iceberg, six compartments flooded almost instantly.

Survivors of the tragedy told of hearing a loud bang as the ship hit the iceberg so, for many years, it was thought that the iceberg had cut a huge hole in the ship's hull. However, when the wreck was found in 1985, there was no sign of a hole. Tests carried out on the hull showed that its steel cracked easily in icy waters. When the ship hit the iceberg, the hull cracked and seawater flooded in.

The wreckage of the *Titanic* was finally found in 1985, more than 70 years after it sank. Dr. Robert Ballard and his team found the ship lying 12,000 feet beneath the ocean's surface. His team returned to the site in 1986 and left a plaque asking others to leave it undisturbed.

However, a year later, another team recovered china, jewelry, and other artifacts which were placed in an exhibition. Since then, more than 6,000 artifacts have been recovered from the wreck. The recovery team believe that the artifacts should be recovered and preserved before they break down and are lost forever.

Dr. Ballard believes that the site should remain undisturbed in memory of those who lost their lives in the tragedy. The *Titanic* Historical Society agrees, and its museum only exhibits artifacts that were saved by survivors.

The Ancient Mayan Civilization

An Amazing Discovery

In the late 1800s, a group of archaeologists made an amazing discovery deep in the jungles of Central America. They found the remains of one of the most fascinating and mysterious cultures that ever existed. The site included huge temples, fabulous **plazas**, and beautiful monuments. The group had discovered a site of the ancient Mayan civilization.

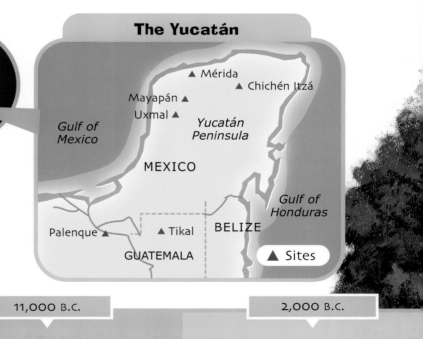

The Yucatán

▲ Mérida
▲ Chichén Itzá
Mayapán ▲
Uxmal ▲
Gulf of Mexico
Yucatán Peninsula
MEXICO
Gulf of Honduras
Palenque ▲
▲ Tikal
BELIZE
GUATEMALA
▲ Sites

11,000 B.C.

2,000 B.C.

The first hunter-gatherers settle in the Yucatán highlands and lowlands.

Village farming is established in Mayan regions.

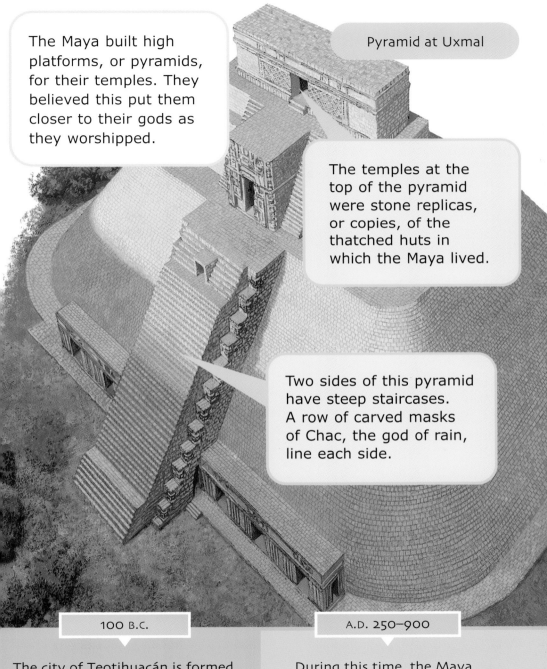

The Maya built high platforms, or pyramids, for their temples. They believed this put them closer to their gods as they worshipped.

Pyramid at Uxmal

The temples at the top of the pyramid were stone replicas, or copies, of the thatched huts in which the Maya lived.

Two sides of this pyramid have steep staircases. A row of carved masks of Chac, the god of rain, line each side.

100 B.C.

The city of Teotihuacán is formed and becomes the trading center of **Mesoamérica** for centuries.

A.D. 250–900

During this time, the Maya build their greatest cities and make amazing discoveries in science and the arts.

The Golden Age

The Mayan culture can be traced back at least 3,500 years. It reached its peak between A.D. 600 and A.D. 900. During this period, the Maya built many stone temples in the shape of pyramids. They had large courtyards where people met and children played. Agriculture was very important to the Maya, and religious festivals often involved asking the gods for a good harvest. The Maya grew everything they needed and often had enough left over to trade.

Mayan Math

The Maya were the first civilization to recognize the importance of place value and the role of zero in mathematics. The Mayan system is based on the number 20. In this system, a one followed by a zero equals 20. The decimal numbering system that we use today is based on the number 10. A one followed by a zero equals 10.

• 1	•• 2	••• 3	•••• 4	▬ 5
• ▬ 6	•• ▬ 7	••• ▬ 8	•••• ▬ 9	▬▬ 10
• ▬▬ 11	•• ▬▬ 12	••• ▬▬ 13	•••• ▬▬ 14	▬▬▬ 15
• ▬▬▬ 16	•• ▬▬▬ 17	••• ▬▬▬ 18	•••• ▬▬▬ 19	🝕 20

A.D. 500	A.D. 600	A.D. 899
Tikal becomes the first great Mayan city.	The civilization at Teotihuacán is destroyed by an unknown event.	Tikal is abandoned.

The Temple of the Inscriptions overlooks the royal palace at Palenque, Mexico.

A.D. 900–1200

During this time, the city of Chichén Itzá becomes the largest and most powerful Mayan city.

A.D. 1224–1283

Chichén Itzá is abandoned, and people begin building the city of Mayapán.

23

Spanish Invasion

In the early 1500s, the Spanish **conquistadors** attempted to take over the Maya. For a number of years, the Maya resisted. Even when they were finally driven away, they continued to fight for their land during the next 100 years. They may have held out much longer if not for an unseen weapon—disease. The Spanish brought diseases such as smallpox and measles, which the Maya had no natural defenses against. Tragically, nearly 90% of the population died as a result of these diseases.

Today, however, there are still more than six million Maya living in the rural regions of Mexico, Belize, Honduras, and Guatemala. Many of them continue their traditional way of life and celebrations.

The Big Mystery

Centuries before the Spanish invasion, the Maya started to leave their cities. Today, no one really knows why this happened. It may have been caused by a lack of food, natural disaster, or fighting. All we really know is that over a short period of time, the Maya abandoned their homes, never to return.

A.D. 1517	A.D. 1542	A.D. 1695
The Spanish arrive and invade the Mayan territories.	The Spanish establish a city at Mérida.	The ruins of Tikal are discovered by a Spanish group who get lost in the jungle.

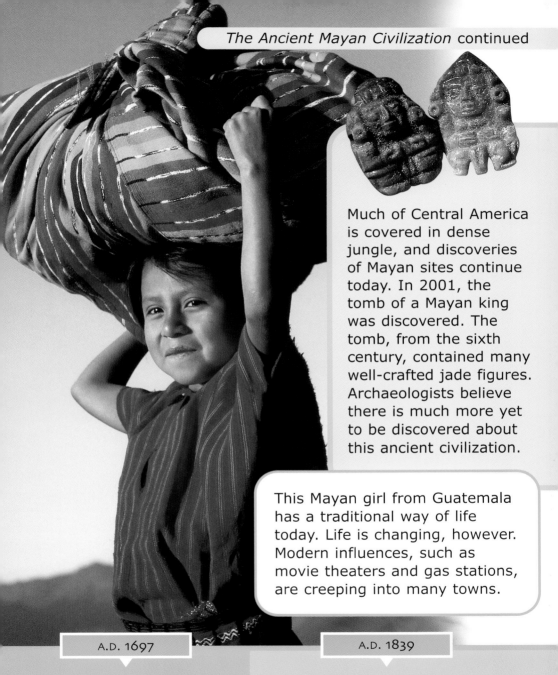

Much of Central America is covered in dense jungle, and discoveries of Mayan sites continue today. In 2001, the tomb of a Mayan king was discovered. The tomb, from the sixth century, contained many well-crafted jade figures. Archaeologists believe there is much more yet to be discovered about this ancient civilization.

This Mayan girl from Guatemala has a traditional way of life today. Life is changing, however. Modern influences, such as movie theaters and gas stations, are creeping into many towns.

A.D. 1697

The last Mayan city is taken by the Spanish.

A.D. 1839

An American archaeologist and an English artist explore Mayan regions and find remains of an ancient Mayan civilization.

25

Preserving Artifacts

In 1989, a new town was settled on the outskirts of Lima, Peru. At first, settlers in Tupac Amaru burned the buried remains that they found on the land. This was from fear that their town would became an archaeological site and its development would be delayed. However, in 1999, an archaeological team moved into the area to excavate. Locals soon began to help the team.

Between 1999 and 2002, the remains of more than 2,000 individuals were found. More than 70,000 artifacts were buried with these remains. The most exciting find, however, was 50 *cabezas falsas,* or false-head, mummy bundles. Each bundle has a false head that is a cotton wrapping the shape of a human head. It is attached to the top of the bundle. Each bundle contains artifacts and the remains of more than one individual.

When local farmers dug up a clay statue in 1974 near Xi'an, China, they tried to keep their find a secret. However, word spread quickly and Chinese archaeologist Yuan Zhongyi traveled to the site. Excavation began within a few months, and row after row of terra-cotta warriors and horses were found. The tomb of Chinese Emperor Qin Shi Huangdi had been uncovered.

Archaeologists in Tupac Amaru remove a protective covering from one of the mummy bundles found in the town.

Peru

Into the Future

Archaeologists have made many fascinating discoveries about how ancient civilizations lived. People are now aware that future generations may be interested in how we live today. As early as the nineteenth century, people began to bury time capsules. In 2001, one such capsule was discovered in an old building in Stanford University in the United States. It had been placed there in 1898. Inside were old coins, a book, and other objects. The items found in the time capsule helped people understand what was important to others over 100 years ago.

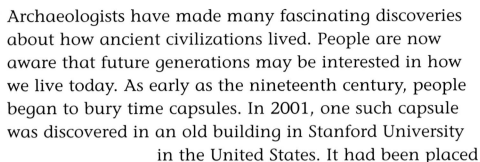

In 1965, scientists placed a selection of everyday objects in a time capsule. The capsule was then buried in New York City.

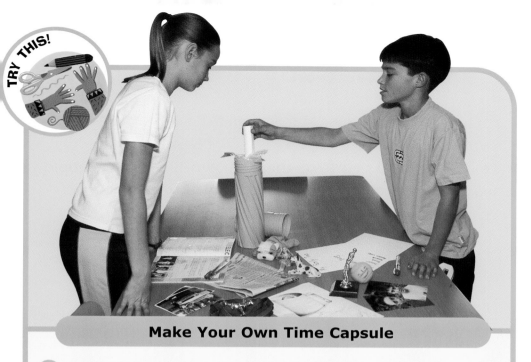

Make Your Own Time Capsule

1 Think of objects that would help people 100 years from now understand what was important to you.

2 Find a **nonperishable** container in which to place the items.

3 Find a suitable place such as the basement of your house or, with the permission of your teacher, a site at your school to contain the time capsule.

4 Make sure the site is marked so that future generations will know where to look.

You might also like to make a time capsule for your future self. Keep it in a safe place. Plan to open it five or ten years from now. Include information about yourself, your family, where you live, what you eat, and the cost of everyday food items such as milk and bread. It will be fascinating in the future to see how life has changed from when the capsule was made. You may be surprised!

Glossary

analysis – the careful examination of something in order to understand what it is and where it came from

anthropologist – a scientist who studies humankind

conquistador – a Spanish conqueror in the sixteenth century. Conquistadors led the Spanish invasion of America in Mexico and Peru.

epigraph – an inscription of writing from the past. Epigraphy is the study of these writings.

Mesoamérica – the area of land that includes Mexico and Central America

nonperishable – not able to rot or decay. Plastic is a nonperishable substance.

paleontologist – a scientist who studies the fossil remains of animals and plants

plaza – an open public area or marketplace where people can meet

preserve – to look after an object and ensure that no damage is done to it

radioactive – materials that break down and give off energy in the form of particles

sedimentary – rock made from particles that have settled in layers. Sedimentary rock is often formed at the bottom of an ocean.

survey – to carefully examine and measure a particular place or situation

Index

Research Starters

1   Archaeology has uncovered many ancient civilizations, but there are probably more to be discovered. Find out about some of the digs that are currently taking place around the world.

2   For centuries, the story about the lost city of Atlantis has fascinated young and old alike. See what you can find out about Atlantis. Where are people searching for it?

3   The oceans have remained largely unexplored by archaeologists. Find out what kind of new technology is now making the underwater search for artifacts easier than in the past.

4   In the past, people seeking fame at any price have placed artifacts, or other important historical finds, on a site and later "discovered" them. Use books or the Internet to research some archaeological finds that have later been found to be hoaxes, or tricks.